Map My Room

by Jennifer Boothroyd

Lerner Publications Company · Minneapolis

LERNER

SOURCE™

Expand learning beyond the printed book. Download free, complementary educational resources for this book from our website, www.lerneresource.com.

The images in this book are used with the permission of: © iStockphoto.com/Kristina Stasiuliene, p. 4; © iStockphoto.com/daniel budiman, p. 5; © iStockphoto.com/weniworks, p. 6; © iStockphoto.com/ Ju-Lee, p. 7; © Laura Westlund/Independent Picture Service, pp. 8, 10, 12, 14, 15, 16, 17, 18, 19; © Todd Strand/Independent Picture Service, pp. 9, 11, 13, 21.

Front Cover: © Laura Westlund/Independent Picture Service.

Main body text set in ITC Avant Garde Gothic Std Medium 21/25.
Typeface provided by Adobe Systems.

Lerner Publications Company
A division of Lerner Publishing Group, Inc.
241 First Avenue North
Minneapolis, MN 55401 U.S.A.

Website address: www.lernerbooks.com

Library of Congress Cataloging-in-Publication Data

Boothroyd, Jennifer, 1972-
     Map my room / by Jennifer Boothroyd.
        pages cm. — (First step nonfiction. Map it out)
     Includes index.
     ISBN 978–1–4677–1109–8 (lib. bdg. : alk. paper)
     ISBN 978–1–4677–1741–0 (eBook)
     1. Cartography—Juvenile literature. 2. Maps—Juvenile literature. I. Title.
  GA105.6.B67 2014
  526—dc23   2012038663

Manufactured in the United States of America
1 – PP – 7/15/13

Table of Contents

I have a hamster. It lives in my room.

My family is taking a trip.
Josh from next door will
take care of my pet.

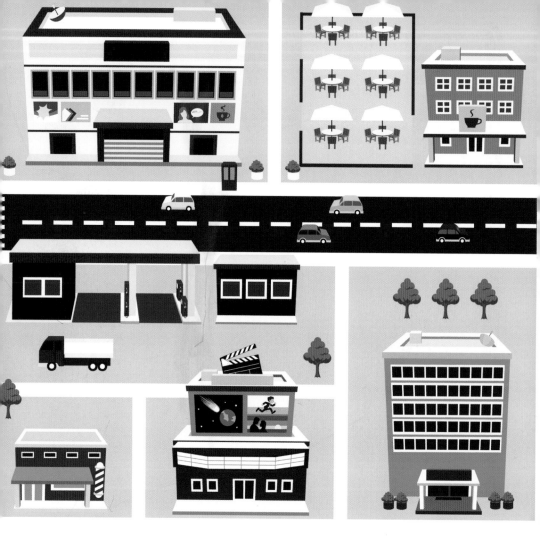

I will make him a **map**.
My map will show where to
find things in my room.

Maps use **symbols** to show where things are.

hamster food
hamster bedding
hamster ball

I made a list of things
Josh will need.

The hamster food is on my **bookcase**.

This will be its symbol.

The **hamster bedding** is under my bed.

This will be its symbol.

The hamster ball is on
my **dresser**.

This will be its symbol.

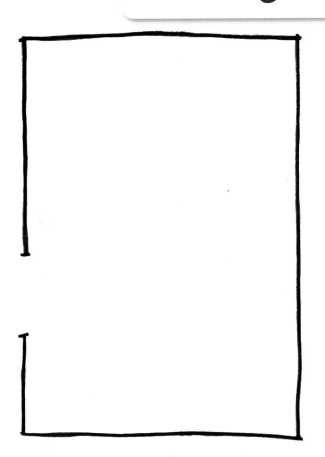

It is time to put the symbols
on my map. First, I draw
the shape of my room. 15

Next, I draw the
bookcase symbol.

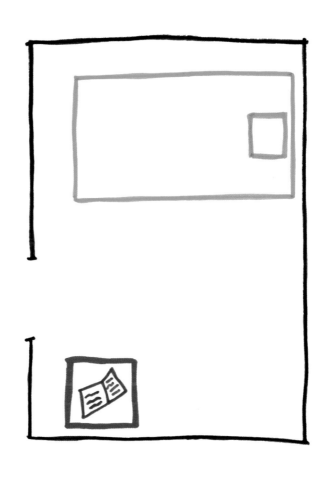

Then I add the bed symbol.

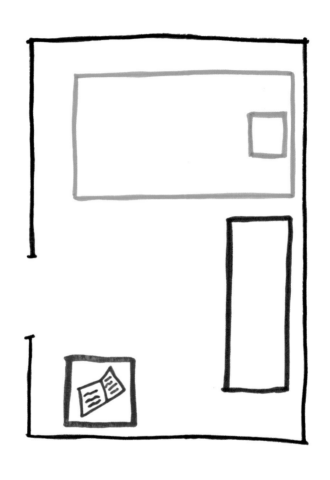

After that, I make the dresser symbol.

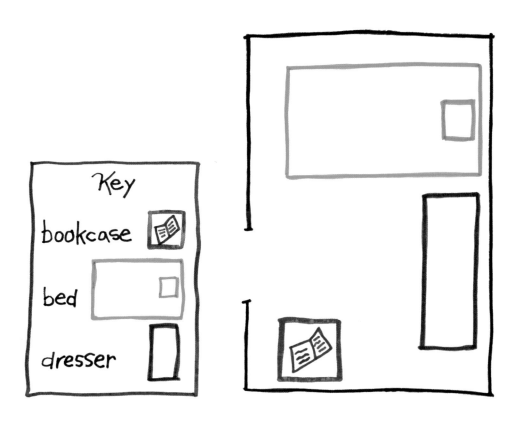

Last, I put a **key** in the corner. It tells what the symbols mean.

19

How to Make a Room Map

1. Decide what you want to put on your map.
2. Think of a symbol for each thing.
3. Draw the shape of your room.
4. Add your symbols.
5. Make a key in the corner of your map to show what each symbol stands for.

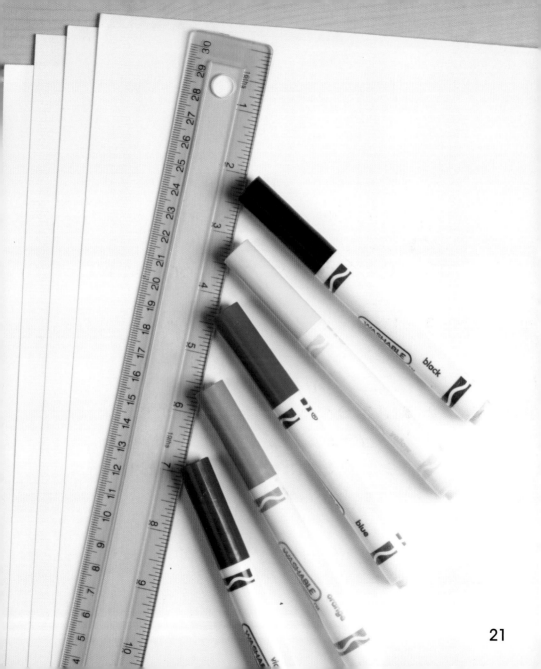

Fun Facts

- A blueprint is a drawing of a building. Blueprints show workers how buildings should be built.

- Decorators make room maps. The maps help them plan how to decorate a room.

- Rooms come in many shapes. Some rooms in the White House are ovals!

Glossary

bookcase – a piece of furniture with shelves to hold books

dresser – a large piece of furniture that has drawers

hamster bedding – natural fibers placed on the bottom of a hamster cage

key – the part of a map that explains the symbols

map – a drawing that shows where places are

symbols – things that stand for something else

Index